21 Housing, Feeding, and Laying Tips with
Sunny Yolks and Folklore

THE ROOSTER DIARIES

COOP CHRONICLES FROM A HEN KEEPER'S
HOME-BASED EGG VENTURE

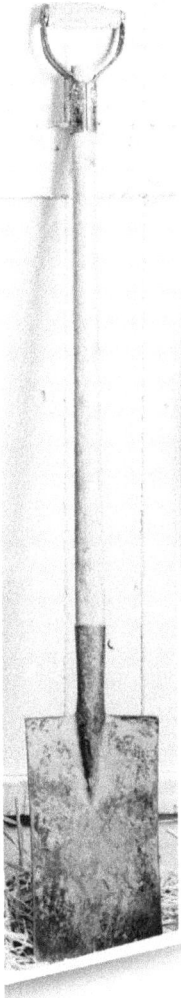

SOVEREIGN NON FICTION

hygge books

WITH A TWIST OF MIRTH

CAROLINE HURRY

The Author Writes

Suburban woman pursues freshly laid eggs and a cleaner conscience.

CARELESS CRUELTY INSPIRED **THE ROOSTER Diaries** and indeed kickstarted my entire backyard fowl-keeping venture. A factory farm is no place for living creatures of any kind. As Alec the Rooster might say, doing a little something is better than doing nothing and just complaining.

The Rooster Diaries contains snippets of my experience with runaway hens, unexpected coop invasions, and keeping the neighbors sweet.

There is wisdom to be found amidst the clucking chaos. Just kidding! It's all chaos! I claim to be no expert.

My forays into fowl keeping have been far from perfect. Many mishaps and mistakes have occurred, but I continue to find solace and joy in caring for my chickens. I thought I was rescuing them, but they rescued me. They keep me grounded no matter what.

Through these pages, I hope to inspire you to reclaim your connection to your food or, if you have the space, to create a little oasis where chickens can thrive, free from the cruel confines of factory farms.

Is hen-keeping the gateway drug to homesteading? Watch this space.

Meet the Flockers!

A quick tour around the neighborhood

IF YOU CARE ABOUT where your eggs come from and want to raise a few chickens in a suburban setting, this book is for you.

Expect tales of derring-do, fowl play, coop building tips, keeping the neighbors sweet, and the occasional "fowl-osophical" musing – courtesy of Yours Truly. That would be cock-a-doodle me, *inclines head* Alectryon, the world's wittiest rooster.

My jubilant pronouncements out-shriek burglar alarms and generators as I hold court. My reign may seem chaotic to the uninitiated, but little escapes my beady eye. I observe it all from my lofty perch.

Am I judging you? I am, too! But it's all in the spirit of fun. Thoth, the Egyptian Ibis god, and the Chinese Ji Gong Chicken Deity share my levity frequency and penchant for puns. A gnostic cock of refined tastes and regal ambitions, I bow only to the ineffable rooster-headed Abaraxis and Mother Nature.

Grandiose? *Moi? Mais oui!* Cocksure confidence is always a win. Men would do well to take a page from the rooster's playbook, but my purpose here is not just eye candy. Oh no, Sirree!

I am here to narrate these suburban coop sagas about predation, tribal lore, and otherworldly creatures, as well as troubleshooting tips about coop building, making scratch food, and hen communication.

Allow me to introduce the good folk who walk their talk around this neck of the hood.

Characters in the Coop

Mem

The heroine of our piece, Mem, has converted her backyard into a chicken sanctuary to flip the bird to factory farming. She keeps chickens for the constant manure and fresh egg supply. Also, chickens – like any loved creature – make great pets.

Mem, who knows a good herb when she sees one, works on the starfish principle – that the smallest individual effort can have a significant effect.

Her heart is in the right place, but mistakes happen when you fly by the seat of your tracksuit pants. From misgendering the hens to not predator-proofing her coop properly the first time, mayhem reigns, but there's a method to the madness. Just kidding! No method, just Mother Nature making decisions.

With the help of her gardener, Muzela, whose deep connection to African ancestral lore brings a unique perspective to the coop, Mem must balance neighborly 'shen-hen-agains' with interdimensional influences, learning on the fly.

Muzela

Rooted in the rich tapestry of Zimbabwean tribal lore, Muzela carries the wisdom of his ancestors in his head and coaxes life from the soil with a song. He embodies the enduring spirit of rural African people.

Abigail

Neighbor Abigail Gospelton has a prayer for every occasion. A sitting duck for psycho poachers, she extends a helping hand to Dickweasel Dan, here only for the free corn and nesting privileges. She's on a rescue mission, but some predators, like the devil, wear their underpants too tight. Will she see the light?

Dickweasel Dan

A pious predator and scoundrel, Dickweasel Dan is a self-proclaimed god-fearing man who inhabits the guesthouse next door. Of questionable morality, his geyser-volatile temper and fruity vocabulary belie his piety. Will karma catch up with him?

From runaway hens to unexpected coop invasions, the road to homesteading harmony is paved with grit, guano, and a doodle cock.

That would be Cock-a-doodle ME! Welcome to the flock.

Contents

Survive the Coop

Predators, tribal beliefs, folklore and unwritten rules

Take a tour around the hood as Smart Alec, the rooster with a résumé, shares insights on characters, coop design, and suburban lore.

Real Estate Rules

A wise rooster chooses a sturdy perch and a secure roost.

Time changes not, but all things change in time. – Thoth

When in doubt, elevate your perspective. My vantage point affords me a bird's-eye view of the grisly spectacle beneath the pin oak: the silver flash of an ax rising and falling. Thud.

A brutal rhythm as the executioner, in his tighty-whities and sockless sneakers, decapitates each hapless fowl on the tree stump.

He has stolen the ax from Mem's toolshed. "Take that, you mad bitch," he says after every blow. Thud!

Blood and sweat streak his bare torso.

Two – a Black Copper Maran and a white Leghorn – run around – headless zombies in an apocalypse – before collapsing in the dirt. He tosses their bodies into a bucket with the rest. Thud.

"Security! Drop your weapon." A blinding spotlight wheels across the yard. The man freezes, the ax mid-swing. A gunshot shatters the night.

There is a cacophony of cries from startled hadedas as the bullet hits the tree trunk. The ax stolen from Mem's toolshed falls to the ground. Thud.

Four security officers emerge from the shadows, cuff the executioner, and lead him away. Lights flick on in the curious neighborhood, and electronic shutters rise from the main house as Mem, the homeowner, emerges, clutching her bathrobe around her.

"Do you know this person, Ma'am?" asks one.

Mem nods. "I do."

An owl hoots. To whit. To WOO HOO!

A few watching ancestors high-five me, too. I've despatched my rivals in one "fowl" swoop—well, six fell swoops, but who's counting?

Go me!

#RoosterZen #Smart Alec's Fowl-osophy

WHO AM I, YOU ask?

Allow me to introduce myself. *Bows modestly* Alectryon here. Smart Alec to my friends. I'm a super rooster with quite the résumé, but those are stories for another day.

I wake the sleepers and add a "barnyard ambiance to the hood," as a neighbor told Mem through gritted teeth. I like grit and take everything said about me as a pleasantry. It's the wisest policy.

I doodle-DO love a compliment. Who doodle doesn't?

I know. I *know*. A spoiler right from the get-go. Sorry. Not sorry. My brothers came to a grisly end.

C'est la vie. Fret not, my chickadee; dying is as natural as living, so let's sing the body electric.

Learn to see yourself as I do – an infinite flow between forms, pure love beyond human comprehension.

Not knowing an outcome is your ongoing initiation.

#RulingtheRoost #AlectryonArrival

For these coop chronicles, I'll begin with my arrival as one of seven brothers in a humble crate.

Better starts to homesteading harmony depend on your perspective. This one saved me from a terrible fate!

My brothers, not so much, but hey.

Mem had misgendered us. In her defense, she *had* requested hens close to the point of lay.

"Look under the tail feathers. See for yourself."

The chick merchant had the nerve to hold us up for her clueless inspection.

"Thank you," said she. "That looks great."

"My pleasure," said he, charging three times the rate.

#HensAndHaadies #HomesteadHarmony

FRET NOT, MY CHICKADEE. The best plans are hatched in chaos. No skilled sailor came from a calm sea. The world reflects the inner traits of humanity. Such as it is.

The chicken industry's foul deeds are well documented. To mitigate these, Mem tries to produce fresh-laid eggs from happy hens at home. Some attempts are more successful than others.

We're grateful to Mem for her inadvertent misgendering. Former friends have thrown shade at her for less. Like all tall branches, she's good at "bigger tree/s" and catches the wind — apparently. As gossip would have it.

Surreptitiously lachrymose – only I see her cry – she finds barefoot solace in our Peckingham Palace coop, sifting through fragments of recall underpinning her family folklore.

Mango-filled wooden bowls and a slaughtered cock for Sunday lunch in the Bulawayo of her birthplace, where everybody kept backyard hens.

The chicken food brought rats, which attracted snakes – rinkhals rearing in the long grass, night adders in baby prams under the scented frangipani.

Her mother found one coiled on Mem's sleeping chest when she was an infant. Oh, the horror! Watch your step. Always look before you reach into a dark place.

She hears her late father's voice in the surround sound of dove coos. When he blew through his folded hands, his pigeon-call repertoire fooled all Columbidae.

Men adept at bird calls make good safari rangers, but her father entered academia with a Shakespearean quote for every occasion. "How sharper than a serpent's tooth it is. To have a thankless child" was a favorite.

The jubilant echo of Hadeda's cries in tangerine skies resonates in her bones. A few exuberant descendants of Thoth, the Egyptian ibis god, moved south from the land of the upside-down trees to nest in Mem's pin oaks.

We take seriously our duties as dawn-to-dusk anchors, escorts of the light and enlightened state. Of course, we do. But we enjoy our repartee with the Haadies, too.

We compete daily for epithets flung over the wall. The Haadies are noisier than me, but it's a close call.

Hadeda Ibises - Africa's noisiest birds

Akoko, Mother Hen

Chickens have been scapegoated since Nyame, the Akan sky god, turned Akoko into a fowl, cursing her to scratch food from the dirt for eternity. All for whispering into the ear of his earth goddess wife, Asaase Yaa, causing her to doubt his integrity.

Akoko's life would forever be one of servitude. That would teach her to gossip like a hen.

Of course, the way he spun it, Nyame gifted humanity with Akoko's virtues – motherhood, protection, and sustenance through meat and eggs.

Akoko, the original Mother Hen, symbolizes care, fertility, and the life cycle. Let's look on the bright side; that much is true.

African tribes keep Akoko's name in their mouths with phonetic variations, including kuku (Swahili), kukhu (Zulu), khokho (Sesotho), and huku (Shona).

If you call your hens with a 'kok, kok, kok,' you honor Akoko, too. Good on you!

#Fowlsacrifices #ancestralcallings #TheNyam

Chickens are still the primary sacrificial offering to appease interdimensional overlords in every country and culture. Some Hasidic Jews, for example, swing a live chicken three times around their heads while reciting a prayer.

Why? The Hebrew word for rooster is *gever,* which can also mean man, making it possible "to see the chicken as a stand-in for a human being."

The kapparot prayer states: "May the rooster go onto death for this person to remain alive."[1]

Some are surreptitious about their private rituals. Others obey their ancestral callings more openly.

One South African parliamentarian filmed biting a live chicken's head off and throwing the carcass into the river told the media: "We do what our spirits tell us ... everyone works by the instructions of their ancestors."[2]

#birdienyamnyam #nyaminyami

Nyam are potent, forceful supernatural river, mountain, and forest beings. The interdimensional NyamiNyami or Inkanyamba clan lives in southern Africa's waterways.

Variations of the Akan creator include Nyaame or the Nyamba. Zambia and Zimbabwe's Tonga people say Nyamba. Nyamuragira, the name of the Democratic Republic of Congo's biggest volcano, means "killer" in Kinyarwanda and Kiswahili.

You don't want to mess with the Nyam.

NyamiNyami, the Zambezi River god, smashed the Kariba's cofferdam in the late 1950s, entombing drowned workers in concrete foundations. The suspension bridge writhed like a snake before unprecedented floods swept it away. Brother of Abraxas, what a sight!

Locals still fear NyamiNyami's power and might. Mem, too, has peered into the NyamiNyami's turbulent, terrifying abyss at the Boiling Pot whirlpool and shivered at the swirling chaos underlying solid ground.

Some colonizers took unpardonable liberties.

They "trapped the river" and flooded the Tonga people's ancestral Gwembe Valley home to build the Kariba Dam, ignoring their pleas and NyamiNyami's warnings.

Today, dead branches from the tallest skeleton trees wave like drowning hands in the breeze at low tide.

Haunted by entombed workers, if the Kariba Dam's foundational concrete crumbles, the resulting tsunami in the Zambezi River Valley will jeopardize 40 percent of southern Africa's hydroelectric capacity.

NyamiNyami will decide when. Tick, Tock.

There's No Place Like Home

Sometimes, home is an iceberg melting into the water, a falling spark, or a departure from everything you've ever known.

Muzela left his gogo's[3] Nyamayendlovu village, about 40km northwest of Bulawayo, to ease her burden. He had seven siblings, and maize was scarce.

Like the Hadeda Ibises, he crossed the "great grey-green, greasy Limpopo River, all set about with fever trees" to seek his fortune down south.

Amid disused mine dumps glinting with fool's gold, Muzela found a minx with a knowing smile who moved into his shack. However, in time, he would learn her loyalties lay elsewhere and not with him.

Mem saw a rare gem in Muzela when he came to her home with a tree-felling firm and tripled his wages to "tend gardens for me and my chosen associates."

Muzela whispers to bees, sings to the snapdragons, and constructs wooden frames for the gem squash, which he labels "James" in black koki on a white plastic tag.

It's a phonetic spelling charm. James. Gems. It's how the word lands on the ear, like Bull-A-Way-O. Mem rolls the sounds around her mouth.

Adapted from the Ndebele word Bulala, it means 'the one to be killed.'

Some words sound better than their meaning.

---

3. Gogo – grandmother or elderly woman.

Mem's vegetables and flowers flourish under Muzela's green fingers. She sends him on an extended gardening course to refine his skills, which are soon in demand.

Mem moves Abigail Gospelton to the front of the "chosen associates" queue, and Muzela now works for her on Tuesdays.

In this vicinity, where solar panels glint from rooftops and generators hum a suburban lullaby, largesse — surplus bounty sharing and horse blinkers — governs the regulatory roost and private security.

The first rule of urban homesteading? Mind your business. Good fences make good neighbors.

#roostermusings #cooplocation

Our Peckingham Palace position at the bottom of Mem's garden is a prime paradise. On one side of our enclosure, a sprawling jasmine hedge perfumes the Spring air heavy with barbecue (braai) smoke and treachery.

Three compost heaps and a ripening maggot bucket infuse the illegally built lean-to guest quarters next door with a more pungent aroma.

Its occupant sure has a colorful vocabulary for a man who professes piety. He may fool his landlady Abigail Gospelton, but he doesn't fool me.

He can quote the scriptures for expediency, but from my branch-tage point of view, he's drinking his way to heaven, one G&T at a time. There's also no shortage of whisky and wine.

From my tree, I see all!

#friendshipfrequencies #thesuburbanscene

To live on her terms, Mem relies on friendship frequencies. Could that be terns? I feel a pun coming on.

scribbles in the margin

Thanks to Mem's solar power, Abigail could recharge her ailing father's oxygen machine (may Marthinus rest in peace) when blackouts cut other lives short. Mem also shares her borehole water as often as needed when the taps run dry.

While they don't always agree, the two women rely on mutual bonds of neighborly affection for harmonious homestead living.

Let me set the suburban scene. Once a sophisticated city enclave, Genteelberg's green patches comprised tennis courts, rolling lawns, flower beds, and juicy earthworms within a more threadbare quilt of informal settlements.

When the pick-pock sets of Ladies Doubles segued into the Parabellum pepperings of homeowners protecting their assets, inhabitants turned to off-grid living to survive water and power cuts. Homesteading became a new hobby born of necessity.

Swimming pools proliferate – useful for filling pails to flush lavatories in the dry times – but vegetable patches and hastily-erected additional dwellings replaced the courts. Who has time for tennis these days?

Political bloat, soaring service neglect, and rampant hitmen-for-hire type crime have ensured a roaring trade for the private security firms that patrol the suburbs.

It's unwise to shake the branches in our neck of the woods, where everything goes faster with a little bribery and a blind eye.

Grease the right palms, and you can do what you like. Isn't that true of life?

#WingingIt #henhouseweasel

I, Smart Alec the Rooster Sleuth, spy with my beady eye, a dickweasel nesting in the illegally-built guest quarters next door. No fixed abode, but self-righteous all the same? Peck. An ex-wife to blame? Peck.

Wait. Scratch that. Legally, Dan is still married to Jezzie, who threw him out of the nest and moved her lawyer in. Another woman. Double whammy!

Now she's his archnemesis, looking to take him down.

From his perspective, Jezzie used to love, honor, and obey. Everything was okay until that wife whisperer, Tess Terfasaurus, stole her away.

Of course, if that were true, Jezzie would not have consulted a lawyer, but he deludes himself.

His fury festers like an overripe avocado in the sun. If he could, he'd turn them into hens.

Too late. They're happy lesbi-hens gossiping and champagne-chortling with their lesbi-hen friends. Dickweasel Dan wrestles rage and inexpressible yearnings in equal measure.

Be that as it may, he must watch his step as they finalize their "undisclosed discovery bundle" to take him to the cleaners in the upcoming divorce.

#throwbackthursday #barrelfishing

Dan hatches a plan. He heads to his favorite fishing pond, the local church social, to find somewhere to stay.

In his experience, the baptismal waters brim with easy-to-net sardines, from the newly bereaved to assorted do-gooders seeking a soul to save.

Waddling duck stout, her face wet with tears from nursing Martinus, her late father, through his last years, Mem's neighbor, the devout Abigail Gospelton, is ripe for the plucking.

Approaching with flowers stolen from an urn, he lays on the sympathy before one-upping her sadness with betrayal tales and lyrics from Women Done Me Wrong songs.

Having spent years prioritizing her father's needs, Abigail reverts to her default motherly mode, murmuring, clucking, cooing, soothing, and squeezing his hand.

Dan responds to her biblical homilies with cherry-picked verses suggesting celestial destiny, even upping her WhatsApp ante with a poem: "Out with the old. In with the new. God has plans for me and you!"

Within weeks of their 'ordained encounter,' Abigail moved him into his quarters overlooking our coop.

"Why, thank you, how kind!" she cried when he handed her a handsome large leather bag upon his arrival. Inside the card was a handwritten message requesting she or her housekeeper separate the whites from the colors of his dirty laundry inside. Woolens were 'to be washed by hand.'

Oh.

#RoosterMusings #neighborlynatter

Abigail is an easy rudder for the dickweasel to steer. She dreams of white weddings, boisterous children, and her father gazing down approvingly from heaven. His last wishes and her faith require a ring before she'll share a duvet with him.

That works for Dan, who regards Abigail as little more than a convenience — a soft landing cushion for his feet while he strategizes how to infiltrate Jezzie's lesbi-hen circle. When he wins her back, he'll make her life miserable again. He salivates at the thought.

There's no way on earth the irascible Marthinus Gospelton would have welcomed the dickweasel into the home he bequeathed to his dutiful daughter.

Over his dead body would that effete scrounger cross his threshold. Yet here we are. Mem reckons he must be spinning in his grave like a ceiling fan if he's watching from heaven.

"I know Pa would agree the Lord sent Daniel to me," Abigail tells Mem over the fence. "He says I've restored his faith after Jezzie and Tess betrayed him. I told him to pray."

"What if he preys on you?"

"Oh, neighbor, ye of little faith, you *must* learn to trust! Dan loves the Lord as I do. He'll marry me when his divorce comes through."

"We'll see," murmured Mem, unmoved by his pious pandering. She wanted to discuss Muzela's African dragon.

My Muti is Stronger than Yours

Home is where the heart is. Muzela's spirit feels heavier than a grindstone. Back at their shack, he finds his girlfriend gone.

His dreams of farming cows and goats in Zimbabwe one day didn't interest her. She wanted someone to finance her every whim, not a 2-minute noodle dreamer! She would find a real man with money instead.

She took the cash he kept in his shoe-polishing kit and flew the coop, cursing him en route with an interdimensional water demon.

For now, he's staying in Mem's staff quarters. When she questions his troubled, downcast eyes, he tells her a huge reptile attacks him every night, no matter where he sleeps. The *Inkanyamba*[4] has sharp teeth, long claws, and horns.

Mem knows better than to crack a joke about hell and being scorned. Or argue with the power of portents. She doesn't question days off work because a hamerkop flew over a village hut[5] or somebody dreamt of snakes.

Muzela tells Mem that the *sangoma*[6] he consulted offered to defeat the *Inkanyamba* for an exorbitant fee, but there was no guarantee. The *musikana*[7]'s Muti was strong.

---

4. Inkanyamba: A massive serpent with an equine head and horse-like mane, the supernatural Inkanyamba lives in KwaZulu Natal's lakes and rivers.

5. Also known as the Lightning Bird because of the southern African belief that lightning strikes anyone who tampers with her untidy nest, a hamerkop flying over your hut means someone in the family will die. Others say the hut must be burned down to avoid bad luck.

Mem tells him to sprinkle salt – he used a cheese-flavored Aromat – around his brick-raised bed.

While the latter prevents the squat *Tokoloshe*[8] goblin from reaching the sleeper, the giant scaly reptile with the horned seahorse head continued to attack from above, three-toed claws scrabbling on the corrugated iron roof before it descended in a reddish haze.

The 11th Hour Approaches

"A water dragon that attacks from the air? Go figure." Abigail chuckles. She's fond of Muzela but scoffs at tribal superstitions.

Mem considered Tiamat, the Babylonian dragon whose body became the heavens and earth when Marduk[9] cleaved her like a dried fish but kept her thoughts to herself.

She sees the Nyam in the Ink**anyam**ba and gives Muzela all her NyamiNyami charms from her Zambian travels, which he strings from twine and wears as amulets.

Not to be outdone, Abigail helps him change his WhatsApp status to "Wearing the full armor of God" and gives him a laminated copy of the Ephesians 6:11-12 verse to hang from his mirror.

Seeing this, Mem, who frequents church only at funerals or on sight-seeing tours, said, "That was kind, Abigail."

---

8. The Tokoloshe is a short, squat, hairy water spirit in Zulu mythology that causes trouble and harm.

9. Marduk was the chief god of Babylon; eventually called Bel.

Her neighbor relates an 11th-hour fable from the Book Of Matthew about vineyard laborers and payment disparities to remind Mem she still has time to repent.

"Why should I repent?"

Mem feeds the wild birds, ferments our scratch food, and tries not to frighten people. She's not perfect, but she does her best.

"To secure your place in heaven and escape hell's fiery torment."

"Which heaven? The seven harp-playing angels or the 72 virgins version? Why should *they* service martyrs?"

Mem views any brands using virgins in their marketing with suspicion.

Women always get the short end of the religious and corporate schtick.

Chaos, Crime, and Cabernet

Mem is midway through her second glass of Sauvignon and a *Breaking Bad* binge when two gun-toting goons in bullet-proof vests barge into her living room.

Her heart is a trapped bird, its wings beating against her rib cage. Walt on the TV is saying, "If you don't know who I am, then maybe your best course is to tread lightly." [10]

Treading lightly is not on this thuggish agenda. Mem offers to mute the television, reaching for the remote.

"Get on the floor!" One thug jabs her shoulder with the barrel.

---

10. Dialogue from Breaking Bad, Season 5, Episode 9

Despite the pantihose flattening his facial features, his calm menace is clear. Your life means nothing to me.

Was this surreal, unpleasant ordeal her eleventh hour? With her nose centimeters from the steel-capped toe of the bandit's police-issue boot, staying present is all she can do.

While his colleague ransacks the rest of the house, Mem wonders if she's fulfilled her life purpose and realizes she has no clue.

What *was* her purpose?

Marketing and achievements? Lawd, no. Eek! What does that even mean?

Relationships? They, too, were impermanent. Nothing she could think of stayed the same. Except, wait. What *was* that indescribable loving presence that came and went?

Could it be a connection to the love source? Was it a guardian angel heaven-sent? It felt like a lighter, brighter version of something she could be. Who was she? Not this terrified wretch trembling on the floor, surely!

Through her terror, Mem grokked a subtle sense of sparkling infinity. When her chance came, she pushed her panic button to summon security.

The private SWAT team could not enter Mem's premises via the locked gates, but their red and blue vehicle lights bouncing off the walls unnerved the bandits.

Stuffing their loot – laptops, jewelry, and cash – into bin bags, they departed via the hedge in our coop, trampling the delicate white jasmine petals into the mud en route. Mem wonders if she'll ever feel safe in her home again.

A Rot Pot Called Janet

Mem eschews offers of counseling in the wake of her home invasion. Why commit to memory a night you'd prefer to forget?

Instead, she replays alternative scenarios in her head, dispatching her assailants with throat kicks time and again. Mem the Ninja Hen!

Visions of them dropping like flies are a finger in the dike to keep the flooding anxiety from breaking down the dam wall every time their masked faces arise in her mind.

She binge-watches YouTubers doing creative things with roadkill and imagines what juicy maggots they'd make dug deep into the compost heap.

Death is a gift to the living. Cycles of life, death, and consumption interconnect in Mother Nature's eternal dance of the observer and observee.

Not a leaf escapes scrutiny, not a bug in the bark goes unseen, and every worm on the ground attracts a hungry eye.

What chicken doesn't adore protein-filled maggots? This flock flourishes on the nutritious fly larvae of our predecessors.

Another spoiler alert! If you guessed we weren't the first, you'd be right, my friend. Victims of a genet-cide, the previous hens came to a grisly end.

That's when Mem got her crate full of cockerels.

A genet bit their heads off and fled.

A genet - wild nocturnal hunter of the mongoose Viverridae family

#FlashbackFriday #GenetJackson

Mem surveyed the massacre's aftermath – the headless remains of six hens strewn across the dirt and fought tears. "The genet didn't even eat the chickens it killed. What a waste!"

Muzela clicks his tongue. "Eishhh, Mem. Shall we call her Genet Jackson?"

Mem cracks a smile and wipes her eyes. "Yes! We'll have to reinforce the coop and get more hens. Muzi, you know what to do."

Muzela pokes holes in a plastic pail with a lid and writes Janet in big Koki pen letters on the side. He fills it with the remnants of the genet's kill and hangs it from the Acacia tree.

Flora and fauna harmonize with their habitat and tune up with the eco-orchestra, allowing Mother Nature to decompose her symphony.

Trees emit biochemical compositions toward neighboring trees to step up tannin production. Antelope browse into the wind before the message can reach them, so the early buck gets the tastiest leaf!

And we early birds gobble the abundant wriggling larvae that fall from the swaying cradle to the ground.

Janet's eco-friendly but malodorous payload wafts through the open window above, enveloping the dickweasel in a cloud of foulness. He steps up the orisons with every capricious breeze.

Dear God! Bring him an ax, an airgun, a catapult sling – *anything*. He'll wring our effing necks with his bare hands! Indecisive, much?

How he takes the Lord's name in vain. What a complainer!

#RoosterRuminations

Do you know spiders and chickens dream? Oh, we do. We soar through surreal landscapes and contemplate the cosmic coop from many angles.

I, Alec the Smart, dream of vengeance for all my factory-farmed kin.

Home is the absence of everything natural for most hens—just a beating heart amid the hum of the egg production machinery that grinds millions of "useless" male chicks into pet food.

In the U.S. alone, over 90% of egg-laying hens live in cages where each bird has less space than a single sheet of paper.[11] Even "free-range" is a misnomer with overcrowding still a huge problem.

Mother Nature does not forgive, and neither do we. Mem follows the compassionate coop design principles of indoor wooden perches and straw bedding in the nourishing darkness to soothe her fury.

Keeping hens under harsh lights 24 hours a day to increase egg production is as mean-spirited as chaining a dog.

We live in a converted hut on a raised wooden platform to deter rodents. Our sleeping quarters contain straw, nesting boxes, and wooden perches at varying heights.

Another compartment holds our feed in a large plastic bin with a lid. Sacks of hay stored in the third section above us muffle the sound of shoes, soapstone ashtrays, and a Canadian snow globe souvenir assailing our tin roof. Random. Mem keeps it in her bathroom.

Humans can access our food bin or change the hay – every eight days is okay – via the hut door that closes with a bolt. A pulley rope controls a hen-sized portal to our dorm.

A second separate nesting apartment, painted in the Tudor style, can accommodate five hens. Its hinged roof lifts on the side, making it "easier to collect the eggs."

Mem has yet to discover that "self-identification" does not necessarily make it so, and her chances of collecting fresh eggs are less than zero.

#MiddayMusings #OrganicChoices

Not everyone has the space for a coop—I get that—but you can still support animal welfare. Organic birds have lived better lives than their factory-farmed counterparts. Even free-range is a fallacy.

In the United States, the USDA defines free-range chickens as birds that have access to the outdoors, but there are no specific requirements for the size or quality of that outdoor space.

Overcrowding is still rampant on certain farms. Everything you buy is a vote for or against your sovereignty.

Nourish the Flock

The more chickens free-range, the more they'll flourish!

Dan fails to assert dominance, a tribal remedy restores Muzela's confidence, and Mem shares a cornucopia of culinary delights for her fowls.

The Pecking Order

Predating on the bereaved as flavors lead in nature's buffet

"The divine bird feeds on the ambrosia of the gods, symbolizing the nourishment of the eternal soul."

– Garuda

AFTER THE HOME INVASION, Mem spares no expense in renewed fortification. Today, security beams warn of movement, a private SWAT team can open the electronic gates with a code, and the hallway flatscreen monitor displays footage from nine cameras installed around the premises.

Mem scans each section before bedtime, interpreting shadows. After some libation, she might mistake the Weber for a pot-bellied blemmye as the hulking oaks shapeshift into a Lovecraftian Cthulu rising from suburban depths.

Are the old gods coming back? Some days, she feels reality shift gears to reveal outlandish truths shrouded in mists of legend.

Mem pores over obscura – ancient maps that show cynocephaly, or dog-headed tribes, sciapods with a single large foot that doubled as a sunshade, and headless Blemmyes, who wore their face on their chests.

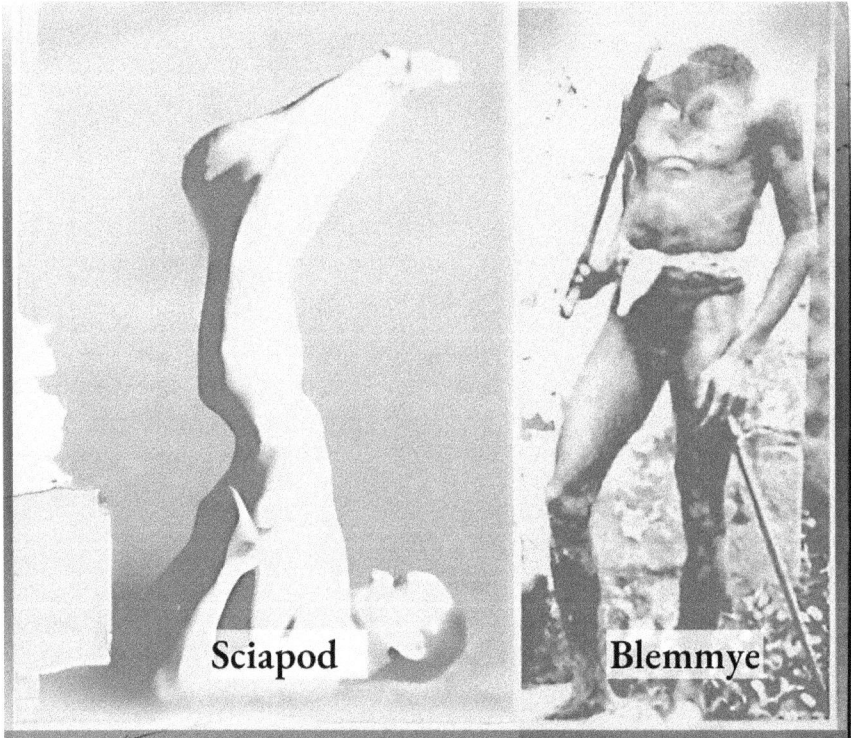

An Ethiopian Sciapod and a Sudanese Blemmye.

She thinks about Humpty Dumpty, the egg man's great fall, and finds parallels between religious stories and tribal lore. Were some ancient gods cannibals? Might humans be stock animals on a farm, too?

Following Mem's reluctance to repent, Abigail had WhatsApped her the verse from John 6:53: "Truly, truly, I tell you, unless you eat the flesh and drink the blood of the Son of Man, you have no life in you."

Mem considers the amphibious Nommo of Timbuktu in Africa, who taught the Dogon people astronomy and let them eat from his body, and – closer to home – the NyamiNyami Zambezi River snake god with a fish head, who fed his flesh to followers during food shortages.

One local Batonga man says it's the tastiest meat he's ever had. He describes a ceremony he attended with his Uncle on the banks of the expansive Kariba Dam to summon the NyamiNyami. Mem sounds it out like Yummy! Yummy!

"The elders drummed and chanted in traditional BaTonga ... Splash! Something huge came out of the water and showed its back to everyone who ran up and cut meat from it. We filled our baskets."[1]

The delicious meat never ran out during the two months he stayed there.

Mukuni chiefs still send five warriors down the 108-meter gorge to scoop water from NyamiNyami's lair to use in ancestral rituals every year.

#neighborlynatter #curiouschortles

If this were a poker game, Mem would raise Abigail, NyamiNyami, over the missionary sanctimony any day, but Abigail takes her redemptive conduit role seriously, so she doesn't say. Zoning regulations depend on neighborly relations.

---

1. x.com/PTChimusoro/status/1772177294724862284/photo/2

Instead, she asks after Dickweasel, who blames my brothers and me for his misery. He lays his bad moods on Abigail, too, as feckless men do.

He doesn't want Abigail. He wants his soon-to-be ex-wife Jezzie back so he can make her miserable again. He can't bear the thought of losing out to another woman, but he has no wriggle room after worming his way into Abigail's home. Boo hoo!

Abigail thinks they might be dating, even though he has been slower than anticipated in coming forward with his plans. How should she proceed?

Mem calls it pre-dating on the bereaved. Like a predator.

"Who pays the bills? You do," she points out before changing the subject.

"Muzela seems more upbeat these days. Have you noticed?"

Abigail sighed. "I wish I could take credit for that, but now he's slathering himself in crocodile fat to prevent the reptile demon's claws from getting a firm grip on him."

"Where does he find crocodile fat?"

"Sometimes, he substitutes margarine or Vaseline."

Muzela's skin has a glossy, glowing sheen. Mem makes a mental note to ask him about it.

Sangomas, Superstitions, and Tribal Lore

In African tradition, the father or guest of honor gets the chicken gizzard as a mark of respect. Muzela tells Mem the one who eats the gizzard eats the whole chicken— the *koko enkuulu*. Now, it's his favorite part.

Muzela's grandmother – gogo – who raised him in the Nyamayendlovu village, 40km northwest of Bulawayo, always got the gizzard. She said children who ate it would grow up to forget their ancestors. He wonders if she invented that story to enjoy her delicacies in peace.

He never forgets his gogo – sending her money every month and sometimes groceries by taxi.

Muzela could not say whether the Aromat he sprinkled around his bed, Mem's NyamiNyami trinkets, or Abigail's prayers saved the day, but life was looking up for him.

He tells Mem his ancestors sent him a new girlfriend named Beauty, who introduced him to Vimbela, an African magic muti.

The Impepho[2] smudging and red Vimbela, she suggested, have worked like a boss.

These days, he still hears the scaly reptile's long claws scrabbling on his roof. He even sees the demon peering at him through reddish smoke, but thanks to the Vimbela, there's now an invisible barrier around him that the Inkanyamba cannot cross.

He can finally get a good night's sleep for the first time in months.

"That's great news, Muzela. What's in it?"

"Crocodile fat," he says.

---

2. Impepho is a Zulu name for a *Helichrysum* herb. *Helichrysum* is derived from *Helios* (sun) and *Chrysos* (gold)

When Mem researches Vimbela, she finds a petroleum-based ointment with colorants advertised as offering quick, convenient spiritual protection.

Who cares if it's due to cultural beliefs in muti or the placebo effect? It brings Muzela relief. He rubs it on his head like hair gel before he goes out.

"I'm happy for you, Muzela," Mem says.

#boutiquebanter #henhusbandry

Dickweasel has been ruffling my feathers lately. He's less man about town and more louse about the house.

We roosters could teach him a thing or two about hen husbandry.

Dickweasel stays rent-free at Abigail Gospleton's behest while he hatches a revenge plan, but men of impropriety should not shake the accommodatory nest.

He would mirror the songbirds in the aviary if he had any sense. Instead, he tightens his blanket of self-pity.

Why do women always piss on his power cable? Let him count the ways. Jezzie and the Terfasaurus, now Abigail, and the mad bitch next door, as he calls Mem.

After talking to Mem, Abigail contradicts his every assertion. She even suggested he start paying his way—as if!

And the constant cackling from those effing chickens! His fingers twitch at the prospect of wringing our scrawny necks. I had to poop on his window sill by way of a warning.

"Why not go into the garden and eat worms," Mem suggested in a pleasant tone when he complained, which did not improve his temper.

#rainbowrevenge #champagnechortles

One man's bane is another's boon. You never have to ask me twice to forage for wrigglers. I *adore* worms.

I feel a song coming on. Yummy, yummy, yummy, I want worms in my tummy that slip down easily. Long, thin, slimy worms, big fat juicy ones, itsy bitsy fuzzy-wuzzy ... wait. Hold the hairy caterpillars. And vermillion slugs. Yuck. Nobody likes those.

Vivid hues and toxicity go together like mesmerizing media weaponry. A journalist in a former life, Mem knows that all that dazzles is not delicious.

The bright orange and black larvae of the Monarch butterflies will poison predators with the milkweed leaf toxins they feed on from the day they hatch.

The gaudy starfish-eating harlequin shrimp and the iridescent blue poison arrow frog, too, pack a toxic punch. Mem calls it the rainbow's revenge.

All caterpillars grow and become something else. Birds eat some, and others flourish depending on their environment. You're always better off following Nature's pathless path.

Plants and invertebrates may not squawk like we do, but they have much to say. The ecosystem shares social signals via mycelium media.

It might be a toxic toadstool in the broadcaster's seat or a shiitake shroom, so only ever eat the ones you know.

#LongGame #corporatecoos #SharpSpurs

A rooster plays to win. Removing it is the only way to deal with a predator or competitor. Some hens are fooled into thinking they can tame adversaries who disguise themselves to resemble their prey.

Always look at what they *do* rather than say. Let's start with the cock of the walk strut.

A confident bearing and feathered finery proclaims his authority as Casanova of the Coop.

Where do you think the word "cock-sure" comes from? Dickweasel has the constipated gait of a man who favors fanny packs and fears being "fleeced by women on the take."

He's never satisfied. Being neither a wit nor an alpha cock, he is clueless about what birds want and would do well to take a page from the rooster's playbook.

The cloak spreading contentment over the fairer sex is woven with delicate threads of chivalry.

Wattle You Find Under Our Feathers?

In poultry, as in life, the difference between cocks and hens is not always apparent.

My kind has a cloaca. My tiny bean-shaped testicles rest against my backbone in my abdominal cavity, generating sperm and androgens, which produce secondary sex characteristics, including leg spurs and mating behavior.

So, unless you're an expert, peering under our tail feathers is not the easiest way to determine a chicken's sex.

Raise your eyes from our nether regions and instead behold the Wattle and Comb development on the head.

The comb of a feathered king is a tall crested crown compared with the more delicate, understated tiaras favored by the ladies of the coop.

While his wattles dangle flamboyantly on both sides of his beak, her fleshy ornaments are more discreet.

Mem knows that now, being a few steps ahead of the average lay-keeper.

Lay-keeper! Lay! Geddit? I crack myself up sometimes. My wit flows from the Chinese Ji Gong Chicken Deity, who enjoys yolks and silly puns. We share a frequency.

Some hens think posturing predators won't eat their eggs or chicks if appeased. They can tame serpents with their charm. They kowtow to floppy-combed fops practicing deception to gain untethered access to more hens and expose our sisters to harm.

You might argue I'm doing the same. Sure, but I'm playing the long game. Courting or combat, my spurs will reign. You can take that to the bank!

Foolish humans. All this clucking about identity is for the birds. You are not your identity. You never were. SMH.

#boutiquebanter #rufflingfeathers

My brothers consider me an odd bird but lack my intellectual capacity.

While they bicker over bugs, I observe human behavior and ponder the profound. No bird is better informed about 'point-of-lay' than me. I'm an authority.

Dickweasel's wandering eye roves mostly toward the full-length mirror on his wardrobe door. We see him preening.

Sitting under the trees with her twitching binoculars, Mem spotted a mystery dame with big hair who looked vaguely familiar but too tall to be Abigail.

Like me, he does not confine himself to just one hen, but is he as forthright? Not quite. Unburdened by monogamy, all breeds and sizes are fair game, but here ends our similarity.

Foul epithets are his stock in trade. Fowl language is mine. We are not the same. He couldn't charm a chickpea, let alone a chicken!

Learn the poultry lingo if you want hens to peck out of your hand. Understanding their nuanced forms of communication is key to fluency.

Chickens express emotions, needs, and warnings through body language and vocalizations.

Overleaf is a quick guide to 'fowl language.'

How To Speak Hen

Boutique Banter: Rapid chuckle clucks convey curiosity and delight. # retailrevelry #girlfriends #shoppingspree

Broody Warning: This is a low, repetitive cluck that discourages discussion. Approach with caution. #GiveMeSpace #incubatingeggs #workingblues.

Corporate Coo: With a murmur and head bob, a soft purr of yield to a higher-ranking hen. #everthediplomat #tediousopinion #fencesitter #peckingorder

Champagne Chortle: A spontaneous symphony of effervescent giggles echo through the coop in a deliciously discordant rhythm. #sparklingwine #finenotes

Curious Chuckle: An inquisitive cadence of delighted exclamations when exploring new territories or enjoying a dust spa bath #weekendgetaway #fabhotel #surprise

Distress Call: A sharp, loud squawk or cackle signals danger or a perceived threat. Other chickens may respond by adding an alarm call to the mix. Never ignore these. #henfreeze #respondnow #emergency

Egg Announcements: Laying an egg is no easy task, so the joyous announcement of success triggers cheers of supportive admiration from the flock. #celebration #femaletriumph #bringersofnewlife

Epicurian Glee: A series of short, rapid clucks on encountering a delectable treat. Squawks of appreciative delight punctuate culinary explorations. #gastrogratification #happychatter

Feather Ruffling: A hen ruffling her feathers can convey agitation, annoyance, or a desire to establish personal space. Respect her wishes. #backoff

Hen Huddle: In response to a distress call or perceived threat, chickens form a huddle, emitting soft clucks to comfort each other and signal unity in the face of danger. #bettertogether #safetyinnumbers

Motherly Murmurs: The soft pacification lullaby hens use to foster a sense of security and connection with their chicks while still in the eggs. #hatchandfollowme #chicksoother #Mumknowsbest

Neighborly Natter: Meeting and greeting clucks when hens encounter each other. #casualcamaraderie #gossipqueens

Nesting Grumble: When hens settle into their hay boxes for the night, a soothing sonata of murmurs expresses comfort and satisfaction. #lowclucks #senseofcalm #flockyeah

Wing Flapping: Like spirited dance floor or sporting triumph moves, chickens flap their wings with excitement or celebration after a successful forage or coop conquest. #waytogo

#matingballet #tidbitting #strutyourstuff

WHILE DICKWEASEL HAS ALL the staying power of a tumbleweed, a rooster loves the ladies.

He mates with the younger hens and cherishes the oldest as beloved companions, attending with feathered finesse to his harem's needs.

The wooing process begins with 'tid-bitting,' comparable to the first few dinner dates. On discovering a delectable morsel, a rooster doesn't hoard it like a miser.

Cooing and bobbing his head, he presents it to his love interest. With a polite cluck, he allows the ladies to dine first and sate their appetites before helping himself.

The gallant cock invites his beloved hens to bask with him in the sun's warm embrace and offers the shelter of his wings on a cold day for warmth and protection.

In times of peril, he segues into the knight of the coop, guiding his charges to safety and standing between them and harm's way.

Let's not forget the courtship rituals, dances, and struts the rooster performs before offering his affections.

He preens and cleans the hen's feathers, knowing chivalry lies not in ostentatious displays but in simple acts of courtesy, generosity, and care.

Dancing is the gateway to connubial bliss, and with wings outstretched, he runs circles around his chosen hen to demonstrate agility and dependability in the *pas de deux*.

He may grab her comb with his beak if she seems willing. The mounting is brief. As their cloacas touch, he releases his sperm inside her to fertilize the eggs. Full of energy, he can do this 30 times a day.

Since we are fiercely territorial, 10 hens per rooster is a good ratio. That's why I, Smart Alec, King of the Walk, envisage my cockwomble brothers transcending their earthly bounds a.s.a.p. They'll have to go once I've accomplished my plan to banish Dickweasel Dan.

Their duel-challenging squawks and posturing are getting on my nerves. I know exactly what I'm missing. Bring me the melodious cackles of proper hens! I need to kick up the Mem-whispering a notch.

#MiddayMusings #MaggotLessons

Ah, midday! The sun is high, and so am I. My spirit, of course. What did you think I meant? My tail feathers reflect the light like the wings of Helios himself.

Which counts more, the shine or the shimmer? *scribbles* I'm a rooster now. Who knows what I'll be in the next grand cycle? Maybe a wiggly worm.

Mother Nature has her plans. Janet's maggot pail shows how fast everything breaks down. And returns to the earth. It's the cycle of life, folks.

The Gender Reveal

While she has yet to collect an egg from her latest batch, Mem has learned the truth about me. Yeah, not so much my contemplations of cosmic harmony as her gender discrepancy.

My brothers and I were getting into some 'peck-tacular' scraps. The coop had become one big squawking, scuffling cockpit. Crazy! Pretending to be meek doesn't come naturally to a prime alpha cock like me.

Our narrative is falling apart since we're proud of our masculinity, but it wasn't just the crowing. When Muzela pointed out how big my spurs were growing, Mem, to her credit, clapped with glee.

"What a handsome cock to cherish and keep my hens company. Alectryon, he shall be!"

Muzela didn't want to ruin Mem's good mood by telling her there wasn't a hen among us. Her sparkling eyes brought to mind a Greek deity.

Not just your average cock, Alectryon was once a mighty warrior, serving under Ares, the god of war, but one fateful day, he slipped up and dozed off on guard duty.

Helios, the ever-watchful sun god, saw Ares doing the horizontal hula with Aphrodite and told her husband, Hephaestus, about the illicit affair. Ever the blame-shifter, Ares pointed at Alectryon and turned him into a cock for not waking him up before sunrise.

Like Dickweasel, nothing was ever his fault!

I can't say why Mem chose my name. Dereliction of dawn chorus duties does not apply to me. We put the loudest Tabernacle choir to shame.

Alectryon's legacy lives on in me, Smart Alec, rockstar rooster, the latest in a long line-up of cock-a-doodle crooners. Did you know every cock has a unique crow? We sure do. (So do you!)

Every morning, our raucous cock-apella featuring my brothers, hadedas, and wild drakes welcomes Helios over the Horus Zone. Or do you spell it horizon? Who cares?

Our combined vocal prowess banishes the night celebrating Mother Nature's might. It's a mighty fine hallelujah at the quack of dawn.

In the illegally built guestroom two meters above our enclosure, the dickweasel neither oversleeps nor keeps his composure for long when we break into song.

Early to rise makes a man wise, so you'd think Dickweasel, *most of all,* would appreciate the volume, but you'd be wrong.

Clad in his tighty-whities, he shoots at us with an airgun for fun.

Feathers flew when Mem discovered pellets in our coop. She called him a fraudulent bully and threatened to tell Abigail about the women she saw through her binos in his room.

"You're delusional. Are you threatening me?"

"I don't need to," replied Mem. "My Mother takes care of everything."

"Your Mother?"

"Nature. She'll always be stronger than you."

"Is that right?"

The dickweasel's laughter brought to Mem's mind a hyena happening on an unguarded kill.

#NewsflashFriday #thebigreveal

With Mem's socialized tolerance for whipped cream on a cowpat, the penny took a while to drop. She even questioned my virility. Such poppycock!

"Alectryon is bullying the adorable hens. I'm afraid he'll cause them permanent harm."

Muzela had been waiting for a good moment to break the news.

"Eishh Mem, those are not the right ones," he told her. Those are boys."

"What? All of them?"

"Yes, Mem."

Oh, guano!

Worm Wizardy

1 Find a suitable plastic or wooden container with a lid. Poke holes in it for ventilation.

2 Line the bin with moistened organic soil. Introduce red wriggler worms. Always keep them in the dark.

3 Feed them with vegetable scraps and coffee grounds. Avoid onions, oil-based foods, and citrus.

4 Harvest the castings by hand. Use this nutritious 'black gold' to nourish your garden beds and make worm tea for your plants.

Then, begin the cycle again.

Produce the Eggs

A Cock-a-Doodle-dramatic start but all's well that ends well

Mem faces unexpected chaos and films the drama. Muzela brings 10 hard-body township hens — finally, a fresh supply of eggs with some cracking production secrets.

Egg-cellent Results

A bevy of beauties take the place of my brothers

Darkness and light come from the same source – the nameless ALL.

Thoth

"THESE ARE NOT THE right ones!" Dayum! Mem could see that now. No wonder there hadn't been any eggs! What was she to doodle-do?

Occasional rituals, like religion, can bring comfort and a sense of purpose. Mem stood barefoot in our coop, "taking root in the soil."

Whenever she feels stuck or in a quandary, she says "calm, open brightness," followed by three more words she learned from Oracle Girl[1] to empower herself. "Undo. Transmute. Generate!"

Helios was pouring the last rounds before calling it a night. She turned to face the sunset and struck a Ninja Hen Warrior pose.

As she did, she felt rooster poo squish between her toes. Oops! Oh, well, nothing she wasn't used to!

Undo.

Exhale. Breathe out all the societal programming. Inhale. Suck in the prana. Hold the pose.

Transmute.

Mem swirled her arms around her head like branches dancing in the wind. And (imaginary drumroll) ...

Generate!

Ta-dah! Mem said it thrice – flashing jazz hands at "generate" as though directing electricity and breaking into an impromptu chicken dance to entice us into our sleeping quarters.

Looking up, she saw Dickweasel watching her from the open window of his airy lair and dipped into a curtsey. His eyes narrowed in a steely glare.

Chicken Poop for the Sole

A good book title reflected Mem as she rinsed the guano off her feet with the hose pipe and closed us into our dormitory using the rope pulley — all except me.

Some nights, I prefer to roost in a tree, as befits my instincts and ancestry.

Mem went indoors, poured a glass of wine, and immersed herself in a raucous election caucus on TV. What a farce.

Socrates once compared the state to a ship being taken over by an uneducated crew with no sailing knowledge. That sounded about right.

The sailors quarreled about steering—everyone believed they had a right to steer, even if they had never learned the art of navigation.

Philosophy will always outlive the philosopher. Stifling a yawn, Mem scanned the camera monitors in the hallway. She saw a motionless hunting owl waiting to swoop from the old telephone pole. A symbol of death and wisdom, she wondered about its portent. Then she went to bed.

At around midnight, her security beams signaled the unwelcome presence of intruders.

Mem counted four short beeps, a pause, and another four – indicating the Peckingham Palace area. Her mind raced. Not those two thugs again! Sigh.

She pressed the panic button to summon her private crack squad security team and kept a cool head.

Had she locked all the doors before bed? Of course. The security now had codes for the gates.

She'd let the professionals handle their fates.

Sounds of a scuffle and shouts: "Put that ax down" and "Stay where you are."

Then, a gunshot. Bang! Mem's bedroom reverberated like 10 slamming doors, startling her trembling Alsatian.

The cats fled from the bed.

Feathers, Fights, and Flashing Lights

Tightening her bathrobe, Mem pressed the switch to raise the electronic shutters and winced at the sight of the inebriated intruder's blood-smeared torso and skimpy scants. Less is more applies to headaches and scaly leg mites—never underpants. What the heck?

Dickweasel Dan cut an outlandish figure as two officers perp-walked him towards the waiting security vehicles, strobe lights illuminating neighbors gazing on.

An official hand on the dickweasel's head shoved him into the back seat of the vehicle.

The djinn in Dickweasel's tonic had persuaded him to decapitate my brothers and me. "Put us out of his misery," he smirked to himself.

Fast asleep in their hut, my brothers were sitting ducks. I watched from on high as Dickweasel lowered himself out of the window and shimmied down the tree. Helping himself to Mem's ax from her toolshed, he slaughtered them individually.

He never meant to cause such a scene, but all hell broke loose when he triggered the security beam.

He threw Mem's ax down after the first shot. Sobering up fast, he looked more subdued, as you do when two burly officers outflank you.

His belligerence returned when he saw Mem filming him on her phone. She'd rue her decision to call security, said he. "That bitch is three scoops of crazy. It's HER you should be locking up, not me!"

"No, sah," replied one officer. "If the Madam does not want you here, you must not climb down from the tree to enter the Madam's property."

Quite right! Mem paid top dollar for the security squad; worth every dime, though.

"Even the Madam next door says you are breaking the law," continued the officer. "She asked my colleagues to search your room for weapons."

They found no weapons since the ax belonged to Mem but discovered a blonde wig and a pair of oversized Jimmy Choos in a box under his bed, which Abigail donated to a Women's Shelter.

#newbeginnings #chickenstew

The next morning dawned bright and clear – new beginnings in the air. Muzela had a small dilemma. Beauty's mother and sisters were coming to stay for the weekend. She made him happy. They were living together, but he needed to provide a feast.

That dilemma was answered when he got to work, and a tearful Mem asked him to take the six freshly slaughtered cockerels. Beauty could make a chicken stew with some mielie pap and chakalaka.[2]

---

2. Mielie Pap – a traditional porridge/polenta made from maize.
   Chakalaka – a spicy South African vegetable relish

"Eishhh." Muzela offered to bring Mem 10 "proper hard-body hens" from his township.

Mem dried her eyes. "Thank you, Muzela!" she cried. "Let's do it today!"

#psalm121 #goodriddance

Released from the holding cell where he'd spent the night, Dickweasel had loaded up the remaining boxes Abigail had dumped outside the door. He had even helped himself to her microwave oven, but she didn't care.

Abigail watched with relief as Dickweasel's bakkie rumbled down her driveway, turned left, and was soon a speck on the horizon. Oh, to be shot of him. Thank you, Father!

Comforting words from Psalm 121 echoed in her mind: The Lord will keep you from all harm. How true. The Lord ALWAYS came through.

Her phone pinged with a WhatsApp message from Mem with video footage of Dickweasel being manhandled up her garden path. After watching his lurching progress, she called Jezebel. Every story has two sides. She surmised Jezebel would be interested.

Mem's footage was the perfect round-off for their "lawyer-ready" custody file. Abigail, Tess, and Jezebel became firm friends. Nothing brings women together more than a common hen-emy.

With Dan's departure, possibility filled Abigail's life again. She adopted two stray dogs, more devoted than "that ungrateful hypocrite," as she told Mem, and threw herself into a new project – creating pavement vegetable gardens for the poor.

#tradingplaces #henharem #flashbackfriday

What do you know, I got rid of my brothers in one 'fowl' swoop! Now, I have the hen harem of my dreams, just as Mother Nature intended.

It's all about cosmic harmony, my chickadee. Embrace your lightest, brightest self and whizz through the grand pecking order.

True to his word, Muzela brought 10 hens from the township, and I, Rooster in Residence and the undisputed King of the Heap, enjoyed the most exciting chapter yet in my fowl reign.

Muzela placed the box on its side in the dirt, and the hens released themselves from their cardboard confines.

Their ruffled bewilderment and rapid curious chuckle clucks as they took in their new surroundings eased my role as their gallant leader.

I was happy to show them around. We hiked the compost heaps, a cornucopia of worms, bugs, and other morsels. They reacted with epicurean glee and squawks of delight. Well, seven did. Three took fright and flight!

Mem and Muzela had to go around to the neighbors with treats to coax them down from the roofs and then clip their wings.

By late that afternoon, when I showed them to our sleeping quarters, they were all smitten with me — as they would be.

As days turned into weeks, the hens' bond strengthened. They banter while foraging or dust bathing. The compost heap remains a favorite nattering spot.

Once confused and bedraggled, they now strut with confidence. Mornings begin with wing flapping, followed by breakfast, hen huddles, and foraging. The compost heaps remain the most popular hangout.

Mem continues introducing new treats to keep them engaged and happy. Their champagne chortles fill the coop with a harmonious rhythm.

#peckingorder #doingmyduty

I'm always first out of our hut every morning, where I wait at the little door for each hen to emerge for a quick how-do-you-doodle-do?! Nudge, wink, say no more!

Hens not in the mood might scuttle past, but I make sure that sooner or later, every hen—young or old—gets a turn with me.

The pecking order is the backbone of any well-functioning flock. With a discerning eye, I watched the hens negotiate to establish the social hierarchy – each jockeying for her place with soft murmurs yielding to higher-rankers with diplomatic head bobs.

One particularly assertive hen, Henrietta, aimed a few sharp pecks at the others, making it clear she would not be trifled with. Her grumbled warnings ensured her uncontested position at the top.

As the weeks turned into months, the coop flourished. The hens laid eggs consistently, and Mem's gentle encouragement and expert care ensured a steady, fresh supply. The egg announcements became a daily celebration, with joyous clucking and enthusiastic cheers echoing through the coop.

Henrietta's leadership remains strong, and her corporate coos and broody warnings maintain order. The others respect her authority. Each hen understands her role within the flock.

Foraging and dust bathing occupy most of our day. Curious chuckles and epicurean glee create a symphony of contentment. A soothing sonata of nesting grumbles and low murmurs mark the evenings as the hens settle in for the night.

By supplying the best straw nesting materials, providing a balanced diet, speaking to them in soothing, motherly murmurs, and providing an occasional hot tub for egg-bound hens, Mem has a steady supply of eggs.

Suggested Chicken Names

- **Hens:** Eggatha Christie, Princess Lay-a, Yolko Ono, Heidi Plume, or Hennifer

- **Cocks:** Cluck Norris, Russel Crow, or Gregory Peck

Stand by for the scoop on coops, food, and producing the most delicious eggs. You'll find 21 troubleshooting tips for maintaining your Peckingham Palace, making scratch meals, calming flighty hens, dealing with Scaly Leg Mites, and more!

Eggy-logue

To rise above the flock, you first have to break free

"Crito, we owe a cock to Asclepius. Pay it, and do not neglect it."

Socrates' last words

#RoosterReflections #MorningCrow

SOCRATES MUST HAVE BEEN a fine old cock, clucking and strutting through the philosophical barnyard. Good of him to think of us as he thanked Asclepius, the Greek God of Medicine, for deliverance from life's pecking order.

It got me thinking about how tall I stand amid the corn kernels and toast crusts. My impeccable morning crow is not just a wake-up call but an affirmation.

Rise and shine! How will you seize your sovereignty today?

#RoosterRoutine #CrowOn

Each dawn is an opportunity to hatch new possibilities. Life's challenges are just eggs waiting to be cracked open, revealing the miracle within.

Whether perched high on the roost or scratching in the dirt, cherish every moment.

Who knows how many sunrises we have left? The uncertainty keeps my feathers agleam.

A young cockwomble might dethrone me. No hard feelings—every rooster deserves a fair shake. I might end up as a rosemary-garnished roast! Nah, Mem would never let that happen to me, but you know what I mean.

We all face the big ax someday, including the great 'fowl-osophers'. Lice, poison, and filth ultimately got Democritus, Socrates, and Heraclitus. Their wisdom remains, though.

Dying is as natural as living. Your current life is the one you release moment by moment. You can rant and rave, blame others, or feel sorry for yourself, but your life is leaving all the same. Let it go. Look fear in the eyes and embrace the free fall.

Like me, you are a sun being powered by love. The current that has always carried you will pick you up at the deepest level. I'll leave you with my ROOSTER Acronym.

R-reflect on nature's path

O-overcome fears with courage

O-optimize each moment

S-seek wisdom in every challenge

T-treasure the present

E-embrace the inevitable

R-radiate love and light

Why did the chicken scan the QR code?

Scan with your phone

To leave a cracking review for the Rooster Diaries!

You're a good egg! Thank YOU!

Or go to: https://mybook.to/XL9U

The Coop Scoop

With 21 troubleshooting tips on building, feeding, and egg production

WHEN IT COMES TO hen-spired living, coop location is everything. Choosing the right space for your Peckingham Palace is key. Strategic placement contributes to our comfort and safety. We want warmth in winter and light summer breezes. Give us enough sunlight exposure and dirt and dust baths. Generous distance from the main house is a plus.

Hen-spirational Design: Happy hens deserve well-ventilated, secure digs with a strong metal roof and flooring. A Zozo hut or Wendy House makes a perfect base if you don't want to build from scratch.

Step up your game with a multi-level perch arrangement. Design it to fit your space and flock size.

Peck-orate With Flair: Use these coop-tivating tips to create a haven.

A Smart Alec Hack

Connect with other chicken keepers through social media groups for legal, coop construction, feeding and other advice.

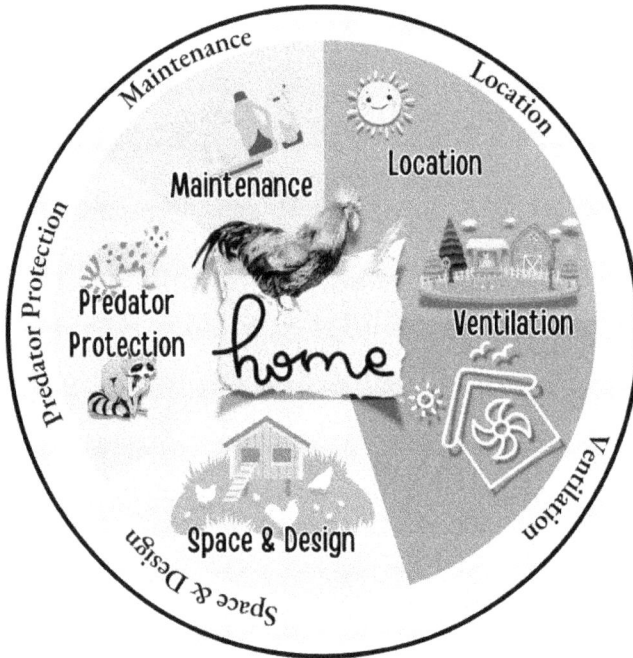

7 Cluckingham Coop Tips

1: Bone Up on the Zone Regs

Don't "fall fowl" of regional hen zoning regulations, which differ from state to county. Bartering might not be the name of your area's zoning game. Get the scoop on local laws before you count your chickens. Scope out their websites for guidance. Eight to 10 hens should be enough for your egg needs if you live in a suburban area.

2. Lay Out the Land for a Safe Haven

Create a good running area with sturdy fencing. Provide at least 3 square feet of indoor space for each chicken in the coop and a run with at least 36 to 40 square feet. More space is always better for chickens who need to scratch, peck, and strut. Ensure adequate drainage. Nobody likes a soggy undercarriage.

3. Predator Proof Your Coop

Genets are not the only predators. Depending on where you live, everything from foxes to raccoons and hawks will eat your chickens. Make your coop an impregnable Fort Knox for your fowls! Dig a trench around the perimeter and bury wire mesh or hardware cloth around the run perimeter to stop predators from burrowing in. Use sturdy hardware cloth or chicken wire for the run fencing. Ensure there are no weak spots where animals can squeeze through. Elevate the coop at least a foot off the ground to prevent predators from digging underneath.

4. Ventilate, Insulate, and Weatherproof

Chickens need room to stretch their wings and breathe easily. Ensure your spacious coop is well-ventilated according to local climate conditions.
Only menopausal hens enjoy a draft!
Coops may need more insulation in winter, but airflow is crucial to prevent ammonia build-up from poop. Spray foam seals larger gaps and cracks in the roof and walls.
Extra plywood protects from the wind. Straw is another great insulator—spread it thickly inside and replace it when wet.
Design nesting boxes – one for every 3-4 hens – with proper ventilation to prevent moisture build-up. Supply comfortable soft straw or wood

shavings.

Your needs might differ from what you see online, so stick to local advice.

4 Make a Roof and Foot-Friendly Flooring

Metal roofs are the most durable. When painted white, they help cool the coop. Concrete is durable and practical but hard on chicken feet. Vinyl is easy to clean. Always cover your floor with hay or wood shavings. Sprinkle diatomaceous earth on the coop floor to deter mites.

5: Branch Out with Perch Placement

Place wooden perches at varying heights in a staggered arrangement to accommodate chickens of different abilities. Chickens prefer a solid, flat surface to a round pole. They sleep according to their pecking order rank from highest to lowest. The highest perch should be no more than 2-3 feet off the ground, with at least 12-18 inches of space between each to allow chickens to hop from one perch to another. A sturdy tree branch can make a good perch, but fix it securely to avoid wobbling. Never use metal; it is too cold for the chicken's feet.

6: Wipe Out Maintenance Woes

Clean your coop every six to eight days. Chicken manure is a valuable fertilizer. Add it to your garden soil or compost heap. Fix any fencing damage and replace worn pieces. Simplify your coop cleaning maintenance. Say no to scrub-a-dub-dub and yes to removable, easy-to-wipe plastic surfaces. Ensure trays under the roosts catch droppings, and nesting boxes can be taken outside. Pop them out, hose them down, and replace them.

7: Work Your Flock in a Porta-Coop

Keep your hens happy and your soil healthy with a lightweight floorless chicken tractor. This tractor lets your hens dig up, loosen, and fertilize your soil beds between crops – a win-win.

Create a simple, portable structure from chicken wire and lightweight wood. Move it around your garden to give your chickens fresh ground to forage.

- Find free PDF downloads on building chicken coops, runs, and nesting boxes: https://www.construct101.com/5-Free-chicken-coop-plans

A Smart Alec Hack

Breeds like Wyandottes or Rhode Island Reds can handle the cold. If you live way up north, additional lighting is a bright idea.

#StandbySupplies

Spray Foam: Seal gaps and cracks.

Extra Plywood: Adds protection from the wind.

Straw or Haybales: Not just for the heydays, both provide insulation, extra warmth, entertainment for pecking, and a windbreak in exposed areas of the run.

First-Aid Kit: Antiseptic spray and styptic powder (to stop bleeding) are good for minor injuries.

The Food Scoop

Mem's approach to chicken feeding blends innovation, sustainability, and a deep connection to the earth. She believes our connection to the source of all sustains our energy – you, me, the cosmic breath, and corn on the cob, being one big interdependent symphony.

Keep your chickens in champagne chortles with constant fresh, clean water and a balanced diet. Commercial feed is the foundation, but avoid food with soy additives.[1] Spice things up with corn, barley, and oats for fun foraging. Toss in nutrient-rich leafy greens, juicy fruits, crunchy vegetables, and larvae for a natural, high-protein snack.

Treat your hens to cottage cheese, omega-3-rich fish, cooked quinoa, and meat scraps. Keep things interesting with sprouts, millet, and edible weeds. Remember to follow the 90:10 rule: 90% balanced feed and 10% treats. Maintain coop cleanliness and secure food storage to control pests. Happy, healthy chickens make for a thriving backyard flock! Let's break it down.

Key Components of Balanced Chicken Feed

- 60 % grains (wheat, corn, barley, or oats)

- 20 % protein source such as fishmeal or dried insects

- 10 % calcium source such as crushed egg shells or oyster shells

- 5% seeds such as flax seeds or sunflower seeds

- 5% other treat ingredients such as vegetables or fruit.

---

1. https://millersbiofarm.com/blog/benefits-of-feeding-chickens-soy-free-feed

Mem supplements GMO commercial feed – it's hard to find any other kind - with the best home-sourced food she can find. Experts suggest sticking to the 90:10 rule regarding feed versus treats – 90% of nutritionally balanced chicken feed and 10 % of treats.

Proportions of a balanced poultry diet

Make Chicken Food

Let's start with leftovers. These should come from a human's plate minutes after mealtime is over.

Never give your hens moldy or spoiled food.

Some farm stores sell cost-effective sacks of rice, which Mem boils with kitchen scraps and vegetable peelings to absorb nutrients that leak into the water. You can include any of the following in a 50:50 mix.

#vegrissotto

- Vegetables – carrots, parsnips, beets, cucumber zucchini, butternuts, squash, broccoli, celery, and cauliflower stalks. Leafy greens and brassicas – lettuce, spinach, collard greens, kale, broccoli, peapods

Instructions: Chop the veggies and add them to a pot with rice and two cups of water. Boil until the rice is soft.

Tip: Add a handful of thoroughly cooked lentils for extra protein. Raw lentils contain lectins that irritate a chicken's digestive system and cause problems like gas, bloating, and diarrhea. Always cook or sprout lentils before you give them to chickens.

Homemade Scratch Recipe

Creating scratch food is rewarding and ensures your chickens get the best nutrition. Corn, barley, and oats are energy-packed snacks that keep chickens active. Scatter protein-rich sunflower, pumpkin, hemp, and flaxseeds to promote feather health and glossy plumage. Mem gives her chickens whole sunflower heads to peck at. Here's a simple recipe to get you started.

Ingredients: 2 parts cracked corn; 1 part barley; 1 part wheat; 1 part oats; 1 part sunflower seeds. Optional: dried mealworms or grubs

Instructions:

1. Combine all ingredients in a large container.

2. Keep the mix in a cool, dry place to prevent spoilage.

3. Scatter a handful in the coop to supplement their regular feed.

The Salad and Vegetable Buffet

Leafy greens: Packed with vitamins A, C, and K, mustard greens, kale, spinach, cabbage, and Swiss chard maintain strong bones, boost immunity, and promote healthy feather growth. They are nutritious and fun for your chickens to forage.

Broccoli and cauliflower: Tuck it on the side of their cage. Let them pick on it.

Cabbage: To entertain your chickens, hang a whole cabbage from the coop roof, especially during winter days.

Carrots: Give raw, grated, or cooked. They'll love the leaves, too.

Cucumbers: Mature is best so they can peck on the seeds and flesh.

Flowers: Pesticide-free nasturtiums and marigolds are good treats.

Nature's Candy

Chickens love a sweet treat as much as we do. Berries, apples, pears, peaches, and watermelon provide vitamins and antioxidants, while bananas boost potassium. Crunchy vegetables provide essential nutrients and hydration.

Tip: Cut grapes into pieces for easier swallowing.

Dairy Delights

Treat your hens to calcium-rich snacks like cottage cheese. Mix in some whey for an extra probiotic boost. Yogurt is good for the intestines.

Scrambled eggs are another great source of protein, but don't give them raw eggs, as this might encourage egg-eating behavior.

Proteins

Enhance your flock's diet with omega-3-rich fish and meat scraps. Dried crickets, usually available from a pet store, provide protein.

Foods never to give your chickens

Five Foods Never to Feed Your Chickens

Never give your chickens salty food. Excess salt burdens their kidneys—less efficient than mammals—potentially leading to dehydration, electrolyte imbalance, and even kidney failure in severe cases. Five more foods to avoid:

1. Chocolate

It contains theobromine and caffeine, which can be toxic to chickens, causing an increased heart rate, hyperactivity, and, in severe cases, death.

2. Onions and Garlic

These contain compounds that can damage chickens' red blood cells, leading to anemia. Continuous exposure may weaken their immune system.

3. Avocado

The persin it contains can cause respiratory distress.

4. Moldy or Spoiled Foods

It may contain mycotoxins, causing organ damage, digestive problems, and impaired immune function.

5. Green Potatoes and Tomatoes

These vegetables contain solanine, a toxic compound that can lead to weakness, breathing difficulties, and digestive issues. Cook to eliminate the solanine for chicken consumption.

If the cucumber is bitter, don't eat it.

Smart Alec

7 Sustenance Tips

Stay tuned for more wormy wisdom and chicken-feeding tips in an upcoming book where we'll delve deeper into the art of worm wizardry and vermicomposting. Until then, watch your flock flourish with these seven sustenance tips.

1. Establish a Vermicomposting System

Creating a worm farm is a fantastic way to provide your chickens with nutrient-rich food. Start by finding a suitable container with a lid, preferably plastic or wood. Poke holes in it for ventilation. Line the bin with moistened organic soil and introduce red wriggler worms. These worms thrive in the dark, so keep the bin covered and in a shady location.

Feed your worms vegetable scraps and coffee grounds, but avoid adding onions, citrus, or oil-based foods, as they can harm the worms. Over time, the worms will produce castings, often called 'black gold,' which can be harvested by hand.

These castings are an excellent fertilizer for your garden beds and can also be made into worm tea to nourish your plants. Once you harvest the castings, you can start the cycle again, ensuring a continuous supply of organic, nutrient-rich material for your garden and your chickens.

Then, begin the cycle again.

Nutrient-rich compost, thanks to the worms

Harvesting worms by hand, 'push & pull'

Harvesting the castings by hand.

2. Hang a Maggot Feeder

Mealworms and maggots are super nutritious and easy to produce; carcasses in a porous container hung from a branch will do the trick. Creating a hanging maggot feeder is an easy and effective way to provide your chickens with a high-protein treat.

Take a plastic bucket with a lid. Cut holes in it or replace the bottom with mesh. Throw in some high meat. Add rotting fruit –melon works well – with a little water. Hang the whole shebang from a branch and let Mother Nature work magic.

Flies will lay their eggs in the meat, and the hatching larvae provide a rich source of protein for your chickens and encourage natural foraging behaviors.

3. Ferment Grains for Enhanced Nutrition

Fermenting grains before feeding them to your chickens can significantly boost their nutritional value and aid digestion. Packed with probiotics, fermenting promotes a healthy gut in your chickens, leading to healthier, happier birds that lay better-quality eggs. Plus, fermenting grains helps reduce feed costs by swelling the grains.

Mem always soaks the commercial grain in water or whey overnight because the chickens prefer it. To kickstart the fermentation process, add a tablespoon of apple cider vinegar. Let the mixture sit for two to three days.

4. Offer Alfalfa in Winter

In winter, offer your chickens alfalfa for essential vitamins, minerals, protein, fiber, and entertainment. Chickens enjoy pecking and scratching at alfalfa, which keeps them active and engaged. It also helps maintain their physical and mental well-being if they can't forage outdoors.

5. Maintain Secure Food Storage to Control Rodents

Ensure your food storage is secure. Use rodent-proof containers and store feed off the ground. Mem finds her three cats the most effective solution for keeping rodent populations in check. Owls and hawks in her area also help keep the rodent population down. Never, under any circumstances, use rat poison or cruel glue traps.

6. Add Apple Cider Vinegar to Drinking Water

Adding apple cider vinegar (ACV) to your chickens' drinking water can promote digestion and discourage harmful bacteria. ACV is rich in vitamins, minerals, and enzymes that support overall health. It helps maintain the pH balance in the gut, enhancing nutrient absorption and reducing the risk of infections.

To use ACV, add one tablespoon per gallon of water. Ensure the water containers are clean before adding the vinegar mixture. Regularly providing ACV can lead to healthier chickens with improved immune systems, better digestion, and higher egg production. It's a simple, natural way to enhance your flock's well-being.

7. Encourage Free-Range Foraging

Mem lets her flock roam in the garden where possible. Allowing your chickens to free-range in your garden enriches their diet, promotes natural behaviors, and reduces feed costs. Insects, worms, grasses, and seeds contribute to a balanced diet rich in protein and other essential nutrients.

Free-ranging also promotes physical activity and natural behaviors. Reducing stress and boredom leads to healthier, more productive birds. By encouraging free-range foraging, you're enhancing their diet and overall quality of life.

Tips for Successful Free-Range Foraging:

- **Supervise:** Keep an eye on your chickens to protect them from predators.

- **Rotate Grazing Areas:** Use a chicken tractor to prevent overgrazing and promote even fertilization.

- **Provide Shade and Water:** Ensure your chickens have access to both.

The Egg Scoop

Get the basics right to keep production rolling. A balanced diet keeps your hens healthy and their egg-laying prowess at its peak. Address any sources of stress, ensure proper coop hygiene, provide richer nutrients, increase space if applicable, and collect the eggs regularly. Regular cleaning and insect control are crucial. Happy hens lay the best eggs. Cluck, yeah!

Common Egg-laying Issues

Here are some troubleshooting tips should the following arise. When in doubt, consult a veterinarian.

Egg Binding:

Sometimes, even the best-laid plans go awry. A hen struggling to lay an egg due to a blockage in the reproductive tract may appear lethargic without appetite, have difficulty walking, or show abdominal straining.

To treat: First, break up a chewable antacid tablet and slip it down her throat on the right side, avoiding the center. This should help your hen expel the egg within the hour.

If that doesn't work, give her a relaxing spa treatment in a warm bath with Epsom salts — hot tubs for hens, who knew? You need warm water, a cup of Epsom salts, and a plastic container with a cover big enough for a hen. Cut a hole in the cover for her head and let her soak for about 20 minutes.

Pasty Vent

Pasty Vent, aka Pasty Butt, is a stress-induced overgrowth of yeast or bacteria where droppings dry and cake the cloaca, preventing defecation.

To treat: Use warm water to remove fecal buildup. Be gentle. Ensure the area stays clean and dry to prevent recurrence.

Reduced Egg Production

Dull frayed feathers and low egg output?

To treat: Up the protein. Give your chickens mealworms, cooked eggs, and fish scraps. Protein is vital for egg production. Flaxseed, hemp seed, fish oil, and leafy greens can increase the omega-3 content in eggs.

Soft-shelled Eggs

Soft-shelled eggs are a cry for more calcium in the diet. Calcium-deprived hens may also eat their eggs.

To treat: Provide a well-balanced layer feed with sufficient calcium.

Scaly Leg Mites (SLM)

These microscopic mites burrow under the scales, causing irritation and inflammation. Signs of SLM (Knemidokoptes mutants) include raised scales, a crusty buildup, itching, and pecking, or a reluctance to walk. Check regularly for mites under our tail and wing feathers. Sprinkle a little diatomaceous earth on our feathers if you find any mites.

To treat: Here are 5 effective treatments.

1. **Aloe Vera:** Apply aloe vera gel to the dry lesions and affected parts. Aloe vera's soothing, anti-inflammatory, and healing properties can help reduce irritation and promote skin healing.

2. **Coconut Oil:** Apply a generous layer of coconut oil (some

suggest petroleum jelly) to the legs to suffocate the mites and soften the scales. Repeat this treatment daily until you see improvement.

3. **Eucalyptus Oil:** Dilute eucalyptus oil with a carrier oil (like olive oil) and apply it to the affected areas. Eucalyptus oil has natural anti-parasitic properties.

4. **Soak in Warm Water:** Soak the chicken's legs in warm, soapy water for about 15 minutes to help soften and loosen the crusty buildup. Gently scrub the legs with a soft brush to remove the softened scales.

5. **Maintain Clean Living Conditions:** Regularly clean and disinfect the coop and perches to reduce the risk of re-infestation. Ensure good ventilation and dry bedding to create an unfavorable environment for mites.

Regular monitoring and prompt treatment are crucial in managing scaly leg mite infestations. Early detection and consistent care can help keep your chickens healthy and comfortable. Implement a deworming program, if necessary.

Pale Combs and Wattles

ANEMIA IS OFTEN CAUSED by iron deficiency or blood-sucking parasites such as mites and lice.

To treat: Add iron-rich foods to your chickens' diet, such as dark, leafy greens like spinach, kale, and beet greens. More natural sources of iron include liver, meat scraps, and fish. You can also try poultry-specific iron supplements at most agricultural supply stores. Implement a deworming program for parasites. Monitor for signs of bacterial infections or viral diseases and seek veterinary assistance if needed.

Beak Abnormalities, Swelling, or Eye Discharge

These symptoms often point to a vitamin A deficiency, crucial for maintaining healthy mucous membranes and skin in poultry.

To treat: Adjust the diet to include foods rich in vitamin A. These include dark leafy greens, carrots, sweet potatoes, pumpkins, egg yolks, and vitamin supplements as recommended by a poultry nutritionist or veterinarian.

Coughing and Sneezing

A lack of essential vitamins or minerals can weaken a chicken's immune system, making it more susceptible to respiratory problems.

To treat: Review and enhance the feed's nutritional content. If symptoms persist, consult a veterinarian to rule out infectious diseases such as avian influenza or bronchitis.

7 Egg Production Tips

1 Wing Clipping for Flighty Hens

Wing clipping prevents chickens from flying over fences, onto roofs, or into dangerous territories. It is always best done with two people; let someone hold the chicken in a towel. Select the first 10 primary flight feathers and trim them about halfway down their length.

Use the tips of these second layers of feathers as a guide. Snip the first 10 primary feathers where the tips of the secondary feathers lie. These feathers will grow back during the next molt. Most chicken experts recommend trimming both wings, but one will do just as well to help them stay grounded.

As in all things, be gentle. Think of it like a canine or feline pedicure, and always use sharp scissors or shears.

2. Early Feeding

Feed your birds first thing in the morning to ensure adequate nutrition throughout the day. Feeding chickens early can support egg production. Also, ensure their water is changed daily.

3. Establish a Routine

Establish daily habits for your flock and maintain a consistent feeding schedule to help regulate your hens' laying patterns. Feed them at the same times – breakfast, lunch, and dinner – to reduce stress and support consistent egg production.

4. Hydration Measures

Hydration is key to a hen's health and productivity. Change the water daily. Add Wormwood herb to their water now and then as a natural dewormer. Introduce fenugreek or a splash of cider vinegar into the water every three days for health benefits. Adding a small amount of molasses to their water can provide a quick iron boost, but use it sparingly, as too much can cause digestive issues.

5. Ensure Adequate Lighting

Ensuring your chickens have adequate lighting and a comfortable environment is key to consistent egg production. Hens need at least 14 hours of light a day to help form an egg. Additional soft lighting, especially during the shorter winter, can keep your hens laying regularly.

6. Share Your Bounty

Generosity is a cornerstone of thriving neighborly communities. When you keep hens and grow vegetables, prosperous abundance becomes more about fostering connections and less about money. Sharing surplus eggs and vegetables builds community.

This approach has always worked well for Mem. It's a great way to glean each neighbor's history and keep up with the gossip. They love fresh produce and eggs. Some reciprocate with home-baked bread or jars of homemade jam.

These exchanges create a cycle of goodwill that makes everyone feel more connected.

7 Keep a Cock

If your neighborhood permits, a cock in the flock offers several advantages beyond our eye-catching plumage, majestic presence, and the obvious charm of our crowing. A cock acts as the flock guardian, keeping an eye out for predators and alerting the hens to potential dangers.

Hens will lay eggs without a cock, but if you're interested in breeding chickens, a cock is essential to fertilize the eggs.

A cock helps maintain order among the hens. He mediates conflicts and helps establish the pecking order for a more harmonious flock. His presence can encourage foraging and exploration. He creates a more natural and stimulating environment for the hens, providing emotional well-being and reducing stress.

7 Cracking Egg Shell Hacks

1. **Soil pH Balancer and Pest Control:** Crushed eggshells in your compost pile or soil boost calcium and help neutralize acidic soil. Place around plants to foil slugs and cutworms.

2. **Calcium Pet Supplement:** Combine crushed eggshells with seed, chicken feed, or pet food.

3. **Beauty Treatments:** Combine crushed eggshells with a pinch of baking soda and water for an exfoliating scrub. Make a mask from ground eggshells and whites to help tighten and brighten the skin.

4. **Drain Cleaner:** Drop crushed eggshells down the kitchen sink to help clean pipes.

5. **Tomato Plant Booster:** Place eggshells in the holes before planting tomatoes to prevent blossom-end rot.

6. **Soil Aeration:** Mix crushed eggshells into heavy clay soil to improve aeration.

7. **Natural Bandage:** Use the eggshell membrane to help stop bleeding.

#middaymusings #featheredphilosophy

Hey there, human in your too-tight shoes, doing the macarena, squawking the opinions *du jour*, and trying to fit in. Take a tip from this old bird and shed that social media grime. It's not the form that counts, but the shine!

References

Chicken Keeping Regulations

United States:

1. **BACKYARD CHICKENS – LAWS & Ordinances**:
https://www.backyardchickens.com/articles/local-chicken-ordinances-and-laws.56147/

2. **My Pet Chicken -Chicken Laws By City**:
https://www.mypetchicken.com/backyard-chickens/chicken-laws/

United Kingdom:

3. **British Hen WelfareTrust - Keeping Chickens**:
https://www.bhwt.org.uk/hen-keeping/hen-keeping-faqs/

4. **Omlet - UK ChickenKeeping Laws**:

https://www.omlet.co.uk/guide/chickens/keeping_chickens_in_the_uk/

Canada:

5. Canadian Liberated Urban Chicken Klub (CLUCK) - Bylaws and Resources:
http://www.canadiancluck.org/bylaws.html

6. Canadian Consultants - Backyard Poultry:
https://canadianpoultry.ca/backyard-poultry/

Australia:

7. Australasian Poultry – Backyard Chicken Laws:
https://www.australasianpoultry.com.au/backyard-chickens/legal-requirements/

8. City Farmers - Urban Chicken Keeping:
https://www.cityfarmers.com.au/urban-chicken-keeping-australia/

General Resources:

9. The Chicken Whisperer – Laws & Regulations:
https://www.chickenwhisperermagazine.com/chicken-whisperer-magazine/chicken-keeping-laws-and-regulations

10. Poultry Keeper - Chicken Laws and Legislation:
https://poultrykeeper.com/general-chickens/chicken-laws-legislation/

11. Poultry Association – South Africa
http://www.sapoultry.co.za/backyarpoultry.php

About Caroline Hurry

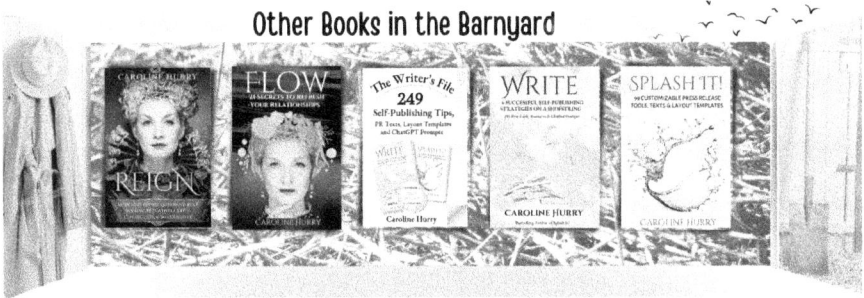

Redefining possibility and enchantment.

From navigating newsroom jungles to scaling bestseller peaks, award-winning journalist Caroline Hurry unwraps elemental forces in *Reign: 16 Secrets from 6 Queens to Rule Your World with Clarity, Connection & Sovereignty*.

Learn to navigate relationships gracefully in *Flow: 21 Secrets to Refresh Your Relationships*. The Writer's File bundles *Splash It! 99 Customizable Press Release Tools, Text, and Layout Templates* (which topped Amazon's Number one bestseller list in Business Writing Skills, Public Relations, and Business Communication Skills) with Write 6 successful self-publishing strategies on a shoestring.

Her perspectives gleaned from adventures across diverse landscapes captivate readers worldwide. More from: carolinehurry.com

www.ingramcontent.com/pod-product-compliance
Lightning Source LLC
Chambersburg PA
CBHW052013030426

42334CB00029BA/3206